GALE
CENGAGE Learning

M000217013

Drama for Students, Volume 1

Staff

David Galens and Lynn M. Spampinato, *Editors*

Thomas Allbaugh, Craig Bentley, Terry Browne, Christopher Busiel, Stephen Coy, L. M. Domina, John Fiero, Carol L. Hamilton, Erika Kreger, Jennifer Lewin, Sheri Metzger, Daniel Moran, Terry Nienhuis, Bonnie Russell, Arnold Schmidt, William Wiles, Joanne Woolway, *Contributing Writers*

Elizabeth Cranston, Kathleen J. Edgar, Joshua Kondek, Marie Lazzari, Tom Ligotti, Marie Napierkowski, Scot Peacock, Mary Ruby, Diane Telgen, Patti Tippett, Kathleen Wilson, Pam Zuber, *Contributing Editors*

Pamela Wilwerth Aue, *Managing Editor*

Jeffery Chapman, *Programmer/Analyst*

Victoria B. Cariappa, *Research Team Manager*
Michele P. LaMeau, Andy Guy Malonis, Barb

McNeil, Gary Oudersluys, Maureen Richards, *Research Specialists*
Julia C. Daniel, Tamara C. Nott, Tracie A. Richardson, Cheryl L. Warnock, *Research Associates*

Susan M. Trosky, *Permissions Manager*
Kimberly F. Smilay, *Permissions Specialist*
Sarah Chesney, *Permissions Associate*
Steve Cusack, Kelly A. Quin, *Permissions Assistants*

Mary Beth Trimper, *Production Director*
Evi Seoud, *Assistant Production Manager*
Shanna Heilveil, *Production Assistant*

Randy Bassett, *Image Database Supervisor*
Mikal Ansari, Robert Duncan, *Imaging Specialists*
Pamela A. Reed, *Photography Coordinator*

Cynthia Baldwin, *Product Design Manager*
Cover design: Michelle DiMercurio, *Art Director*
Page design: Pamela A. E. Galbreath, *Senior Art Director*

ISSN applied for and pending

Printed in the United States of America
10 9 8 7 6 5 4 3

Pygmalion

George Bernard Shaw

1914

Pygmalion is a comedy about a phonetics expert who, as a kind of social experiment, attempts to make a lady out of an uneducated Cockney flower-girl. Although not as intellectually complex as some of the other plays in Shaw's "theatre of ideas," *Pygmalion* nevertheless probes important questions about social class, human behavior, and relations between the sexes.

Hoping to circumvent what he felt was the

tendency of the London press to criticize his plays unfairly, Shaw chose to produce a German translation of *Pygmalion* in Vienna and Berlin before bringing the play to London. The London critics appreciated the acclaim the play had received overseas, and, after it opened at His Majesty's Theatre on April 11, 1914, it enjoyed success, firmly establishing Shaw's reputation as a popular playwright.

Accompanying his subterfuge with the London press, Shaw also plotted to trick his audience out of any prejudicial views they held about the play's content. This he did by assuming their familiarity with the myth of Pygmalion, from the Greek playwright Ovid's *Metamorphoses,* encouraging them to think that *Pygmalion* was a classical play. He furthered the ruse by directing the play anonymously and casting a leading actress who had never before appeared in a working-class role. In Ovid's tale, Pygmalion is a man disgusted with real-life women who chooses celibacy and the pursuit of an ideal woman, whom he carves out of ivory. Wishing the statue were real, he makes a sacrifice to Venus, the goddess of love, who brings the statue to life. By the late Renaissance, poets and dramatists began to contemplate the thoughts and feelings of this woman, who woke full-grown in the arms of a lover. Shaw's central character—the flower girl Liza Doolittle—expresses articulately how her transformation has made her feel, and he adds the additional twist that Liza turns on her "creator" in the end by leaving him.

In addition to the importance of the original Pygmalion myth to Shaw's play, critics have pointed out the possible influence of other works, such as Tobias Smollett's novel *The Adventures of Peregrine Pickle* (which similarly involves a gentleman attempting to make a fine lady out of a "coarse" working girl), and a number of plays, including W.S. Gilbert's *Pygmalion and Galatea* and Henrik Ibsen's *A Doll House*. Shaw denied borrowing the story directly from any of these sources, but there are traces of them in his play, as there are of the well-known story of Cinderella, and shades of the famous stories of other somewhat vain "creators" whose experiments have unforeseen implications: Faust, Dr. Frankenstein, Svengali.

The play was viewed (thankfully, by many critics) as one of Shaw's less provocative comedies. Nevertheless, *Pygmalion* did provoke controversy upon its original production. Somewhat ironically, the cause was an issue of language, around which the plot itself turns: Liza's use of the word "bloody," never before uttered on the stage at His Majesty's Theatre. Even though they were well aware of the controversy from its coverage in the press, the first audiences gasped in surprise, then burst into laughter, at Liza's spirited rejoinder: "Not bloody likely!"

Author Biography

George Bernard Shaw was born into a poor Protestant family in Dublin, Ireland, on July 26, 1856. Despite childhood neglect (his father was an alcoholic), he became one of the most prominent writers of modern Britain. His mother introduced him to music and art at an early age and after 1876, when he moved to London to continue his self-education, she supported him for nine more years. During this period Shaw wrote five unsuccessful novels, then, in 1884, he met William Archer, the prominent journalist and drama critic, who urged him to write plays. Through Archer, Shaw became music critic for a London newspaper. With a strong background in economics and politics, Shaw rose to prominence through the socialist Fabian Society, which he helped organize in 1884. He also established himself as a persuasive orator and became well known as a critic of art, music, and literature. In 1895 he became the drama critic for the *Saturday Review*.

Shaw's socialist viewpoint and penetrating wit show through in his journalism, economic and political tracts, and his many plays. An articulate nonconformist, Shaw believed in a spirit he called the Life Force that would help improve and eventually perfect the world. This hope for human and social improvement gave a sense of purpose to much of Shaw's work and had a broad range of effects across many facets of his life, from his vegetarian diet to his satirizing of social pretensions. It also led to his rebellion against the prevailing idea of "art for art's sake" (that is, works of art that did not also have an explicit social purpose).

Shaw's plays were frequently banned by censors or refused production (both their themes and their expansive scope made them difficult to stage), so he sought audiences through open readings and publication. He published his first collection, *Plays Pleasant and Unpleasant,* in 1898, which included the combative, "unpleasant" works *Widowers' Houses* (his first play), *Mrs. Warren's Profession,* and *The Philanderer;* and the milder, more tongue-in-cheek plays *Arms and the Man, Candida, The Man of Destiny,* and *You Never Can Tell.* Also in 1898, Shaw married the wealthy Charlotte Payne-Townsend. The year was a turning point in Shaw's life, after which he was centrally associated with the intellectual revival of the English theatre.

After the turn of the century, Shaw's plays gradually began to achieve production and, eventually, acceptance in England. Throughout his long life, his work expressed a mischievous delight in outstripping ponderous intellectual institutions. His subsequent plays include *Man and Superman* (written from 1901 to 1903), a complex idea play about human capability; *John Bull's Other Island* (1904), a satire of British opinions concerning his native Ireland; *Major Barbara* (1905), a dazzling investigation of social conscience and reform;

Pygmalion (1914); *Heartbreak House* (1920), an anguished allegory of Europe before the First World War;

Back to Methuselah (1922), a legend cycle for Shaw's "religion" of creative evolution; *Saint Joan* (1923), a startling historical tragedy; *The Apple Cart* (1929), one of three later plays Shaw termed "political extravaganzas"; and *Buoyant Billions* (1948), his last full-length play.

Shaw received the Nobel Prize for literature in 1925, which was considered to be the high point of his career (although he was still to write seventeen more plays). In later life, he remained a vigorous symbol of the ageless superman he proclaimed in his works, traveling extensively throughout the world and engaging in intellectual and artistic pursuits. In September, 1950, however, he fell from an apple tree he was pruning, and on November 2 of that year died of complications stemming from the injury.

Plot Summary

Act I

The action begins at 11:15 p.m. in a heavy summer rainstorm. An after-theatre crowd takes shelter in the portico of St. Paul's Church in Covent Garden. A young girl, Clara Eynsford Hill, and her mother are waiting for Clara's brother Freddy, who looks in vain for an available cab. Colliding into flower peddler Liza Doolittle, Freddy scatters her flowers. After he departs to continue looking for a cab, Liza convinces Mrs. Eynsford Hill to pay for the damaged flowers; she then cons three halfpence from Colonel Pickering. Liza is made aware of the presence of Henry Higgins, who has been writing down every word she has said. Thinking Higgins is a policeman who is going to arrest her for scamming people, Liza becomes hysterical. Higgins turns out, however, to be making a record of her speech for scientific ends. Higgins is an expert in phonetics who claims: "I can place any man within six miles. I can place him within two miles in London. Sometimes within two streets." Upbraiding Liza for her speech, Higgins boasts that "in three months I could pass that girl off as a duchess at an ambassador's garden party." Higgins and Pickering eventually trade names and realize they have long wanted to meet each other. They go off to dine together and discuss phonetics. Liza picks up the money Higgins had flung down upon exiting and for once treats herself to a taxi ride home.

Act II

The next morning at 11 a.m. in Higgins's laboratory, which is full of instruments. Higgins and Pickering receive Liza, who has presented herself at the door. Higgins is taken aback by Liza's request for lessons from him. She wants to learn to "talk more genteel" so she can be employed in a flower shop instead of selling flowers on the street. Liza can only offer to pay a shilling per lesson, but Pickering, intrigued by Higgins's claims the previous night, offers to pay for Liza's lessons and says of the experiment: "I'll say you're the greatest teacher alive if you make that good." Higgins enthusiastically accepts the bet, though his housekeeper, Mrs. Pearce, pleads with him to consider what will become of Liza after the experiment. Liza agrees to move into Higgins's home and goes upstairs for a bath. Meanwhile, Higgins and Pickering are visited by Liza's father, Doolittle, "an elderly but vigorous dustman." Rather than demanding to take Liza away, Doolittle instead offers to "let her go" for the sum of five pounds. Higgins is shocked by this offer at first, asking whether Doolittle has any morals, but he is persuaded by Doolittle's response, that the latter is too poor to afford them. Exiting quickly with his booty, Doolittle does not at first recognize his daughter, who has re-entered, cleaned up and dressed in a Japanese kimono.

Act III

The setting is the flat of Mrs. Higgins, Henry's mother. Henry bursts in with a flurry of excitement, much to the distress of his mother, who finds him lacking in social graces (she observes that her friends "stop coming whenever they meet you"). Henry explains that he has invited Liza, taking the opportunity for an early test of his progress with Liza's speech. The Eynsford Hills, guests of Mrs. Higgins, arrive. The discussion is awkward and Henry, true to his mother's observations, does appear very uncomfortable in company. Liza arrives and, while she speaks with perfect pronunciation and tone, she confuses the guests with many of her topics of conversation and peculiar turns of phrase. Higgins convinces the guests that these, including Liza's famous exclamation "not bloody likely!" are the latest trend in small talk. After all the guests (including Liza) have left, Mrs. Higgins challenges Henry and Pickering regarding their plans; she is shocked that they have given no thought to Liza's well-being, for after the conclusion of the experiment she will have no income, only "the manners and habits that disqualify a fine lady from earning her own living." Henry is characteristically flip, stating "there's no good bothering now. The thing's done." Pickering is no more thoughtful than Higgins, and as the two men exit, Mrs. Higgins expresses her exasperation.

A following scene, the most important of the "optional" scenes Shaw wrote for the film version of *Pygmalion*—and included in later editions of the play—takes place at an Embassy party in London. Higgins is nervous that Nepommuck, a Hungarian interpreter and his former student, will discover his ruse and expose Liza as an aristocratic imposter. Nepommuck, ironically, accuses Liza not of faking her social class, but her nationality. He is convinced Liza must be Hungarian and of noble blood, for she speaks English "too perfectly," and "only foreigners who have been taught to speak it speak it well." Higgins is victorious, but finds little pleasure in having outwitted such foolish guests.

Act IV

Midnight, in Henry's laboratory. Higgins, Pickering, and Liza return from the party. Higgins loudly bemoans the evening:"What a crew! What a silly tomfoolery!" Liza grows more and more frustrated as he continues to complain ("Thank God it's over!"), not paying attention to her or acknowledging her role in his triumph. Complaining about not being able to find his slippers, Higgins does not observe Liza retrieving them and placing them directly by him. She controls her anger as Higgins and Pickering exit, but when Higgins storms back in, still wrathfully looking for his slippers, Liza hurls them at him with all her might. She derides Higgins for his selfishness and demands of him, "What's to become of me?" Higgins tries to convince her that her irritation is "only imagination," that she should "go to bed like a good girl and sleep it off." Higgins gradually understands Liza's economic concern (that she cannot go back to selling flowers, but has no other future), but he can only awkwardly suggest marriage to a rich man as a solution. Liza criticizes the subjugation that Higgins's suggestion implies: "I sold flowers. I didn't sell myself. Now you've made a lady of me I'm not fit to sell anything else." Liza infuriates Higgins by rejecting him, giving him back the rented jewels she wears, and a ring he had bought for her. He angrily throws the ring in the fireplace and storms out.

In the next important "optional scene," Liza has left Higgins's home and comes upon Freddy, who, infatuated with the former flower girl, has recently been spending most of his nights gazing up at Liza's window. They fall into each other's arms, but their passionate kisses are interrupted first by one constable, then another, and another. Liza suggests they jump in a taxi, "and drive about all night; and in the morning I'll call on old Mrs Higgins and ask her what I ought to do."

Act V

Mrs. Higgins's drawing room, the next day. Henry and Pickering arrive and while they are downstairs phoning the police about Liza's disappearance, Mrs. Higgins asks the chambermaid to warn Liza, taking shelter upstairs, not to come down. Mrs. Higgins scolds Henry and Pickering for their childishness and the careless manner in which they treated another human. The arrival of Alfred Doolittle is announced; he enters dressed fashionably as a bridegroom, but in an agitated state, casting accusations at Higgins. Doolittle explains at length how by a deed of Henry's he has come into a regular pension. His lady companion will now marry him, but still he is miserable. Where he once could "put the touch" on anyone for drinking money, now everyone comes to him, demanding favors and monetary support. At this point, Mrs. Higgins reveals that Liza is upstairs, again criticizing Henry for his unthoughtful behavior towards the girl. Mrs. Higgins calls Liza down, asking Doolittle to step out for a moment to delay the shock of the news he brings. Liza enters, politely cool towards Henry. She thanks Pickering for all the respect he has shown her since their first meeting: calling her Miss Doolittle, removing his hat, opening doors. "The difference," Liza concludes, "between a lady and a flower girl is not how she behaves but how she's treated."

At this point, Doolittle returns. He and Liza are re-united, and all the characters (excepting Henry) prepare to leave to see Doolittle married. Liza and Higgins are left alone. Higgins argues that he didn't treat Liza poorly because she was a flower girl but because he treats everyone the same. He defends his behavior by attacking traditional social graces as absurd: "You call me a brute because you couldn't buy a claim on me by fetching my slippers," he says. Liza declares that since Higgins gave no thought to her future, she will marry Freddy and support herself by teaching phonetics, perhaps assisting Nepommuck. Higgins grows furious at Liza and "lays his hands on her." He quickly regrets doing so and expresses appreciation of Liza's newfound independence. At the play's curtain he remains incorrigible, however, cheerfully assuming that Liza will continue to manage his household details as she had done during her days of instruction with him.

Characters

Clara

See Miss Clara Eynsford Hill

Doolittle

See Alfred Doolittle

Alfred Doolittle

Alfred is Liza's father, whom Shaw describes as "an elderly but vigorous dustman. . . . He has well marked and rather interesting features, and seems equally free from fear or conscience. He has a remarkably expressive voice, the result of a habit of giving vent to his feelings without reserve." Doolittle describes himself as the "undeserving poor," who need just as much as the deserving but never get anything because of the disapproval of middle-class morality. Nevertheless, he is a skilled moocher who is capable of finessing loans from the most miserly of people. He is miserable when he comes into money during the course of the play, however, because people then come with hopes of borrowing money.

Eliza Doolittle

A cockney flower girl of around 18 or 20 years of age, Eliza is streetwise and energetic. She is not educated by traditional standards, but she is intelligent and a quick learner. As she presents herself in her "shoddy coat" at Higgins's laboratory, Shaw describes the "pathos of this deplorable figure, with its innocent vanity and consequential air." She learns a genteel accent from Higgins and, washed and dressed exquisitely, passes in society for a Duchess. In this transformed state, she is shown to be capable of inspiring awe in the observer. While she wins Higgins's wager for him, she is shocked to find him lose interest in her once the experiment is complete; she cannot believe that he's given no thought to her future well-being. Pickering, by having been polite to her from the very beginning, provides a contrast, from which Liza is able to realize that "the difference between a lady and a flower girl is not how she behaves, but how she's treated." She learns from Higgins's behavior an even deeper truth, that social graces and class are not the true measure of a person's worth.

Media Adaptations

- *Pygmalion* was adapted as a film produced by Gabriel Pascal, directed by Anthony Asquith and Leslie Howard, starring Howard and Wendy Hiller; Metro-Goldwyn-Mayer, 1938. The film received Academy Awards for Shaw's screenplay and for the adaptation by Ian Dalrymple, Cecil Lewis, and W. P. Lipscomb.

- *Pygmalion* was also filmed for American television, directed by George Schaefer for the Hallmark Hall of Fame series, starring Julie Harris and James Donald, adapted by Robert Hartung; Compass, 1963.

- The play has also been produced in audio recordings. In 1972 Peter

Wood directed a recording starring Michael Redgrave, Donald Pleasence, and Lynn Redgrave (Caedmon TRS 354). In 1974, the play was recorded in association with the British Council, starring Alec McCowen and Diana Rigg (Argo SAY 28).

- *Pygmalion* was also adapted into the musical *My Fair Lady* by Alan Jay Lerner and Frederick Loewe. An original cast recording was released in 1959, starring Rex Harrison, Julie Andrews, and Stanley Holloway (CK 2015 Columbia).

- *My Fair Lady* was made into a film in 1964, produced by Jack L. Warner and directed by George Cukor, starring Audrey Hepburn as Liza with Rex Harrison reprising his stage role of Higgins. The film was nominated for twelve Academy Awards and received eight. It is considered a film classic in the musical genre.

Miss Doolittle

See Eliza Doolittle

Freddy

See Frederick Eynsford Hill

Henry Higgins

Henry Higgins is an expert in phonetics and the author of "Higgins's Universal Alphabet." Shaw describes him as "a robust, vital, appetizing sort of man of forty or thereabouts. . . . He is of the energetic, scientific type, heartily, even violently interested in everything that can be studied as a scientific subject, and careless about himself and other people, including their feelings. . . . His manner varies from genial bullying. . . to stormy petulance. . . but he is so entirely frank and void of malice that he remains likeable even in his least reasonable moments." In his book *Shaw: The Plays,* Desmond MacCarthy observed that "Higgins is called a professor of phonetics, but he is really an artist—that is the interesting thing about him, and his character is a study of the creative temperament."

For many, this temperament is a difficult one. His housekeeper, Mrs. Pearce, observes of Higgins that "when you get what you called interested in people's accents, you never think of what may happen to them or you." Certainly, Higgins gives no thought to Liza's future after his experiment, and when he gradually loses interest in it, he seems, at least from her perspective, to have disposed of her as well. He is shaken by the independence Liza demonstrates and thus by the end of the play is able to show a kind of respect to her. It is on such terms and presented in such a way, however, that a romantic ending between himself and Liza is never really feasible.

Mrs. Higgins

Henry's mother, a generous and gracious woman. She is frequently exasperated by her son's lack of manners and completely sympathizes with Liza when the girl leaves Higgins and takes shelter with her. She is perceptive and intelligent, and capable of putting Henry in his place. It is indicative of Mrs. Higgins's character that after the conflict between her son and Liza, both characters choose to come to her for guidance.

Frederick Eynsford Hill

Freddy is an upper-class young man of around 20, somewhat weak although eager and good-natured. Proper and upstanding, he is infatuated with Liza and thoroughly devoted to her both before and after she takes shelter with him in an all-night cab after leaving Higgins. Liza claims to be going back to him at the end of the play, an idea which Higgins finds preposterous. Freddy does not have the money to support them both (and from Liza's perspective seems unfit for difficult work), which prompts her idea to earn a living by teaching phonetics.

Miss Clara Eynsford Hill

A pampered socialite of around 20, she is somewhat gullible and easily disgusted. Shaw writes that she "has acquired a gay air of being very much at home in society; the bravado of genteel poverty." Her social position is not secured, however, and this anxiety drives much of her behavior.

Mrs. Eynsford Hill

The middle-aged mother of Freddy and Clara, whom Shaw describes as "well-bred, quiet" and having "the habitual anxiety of straitened means." She is acutely aware of social decorum and highly invested in finding proper spouses for her two children.

Liza

See Eliza Doolittle

Nepommuck

Higgins's first pupil and later his dupe, a Hungarian of around 30. The mustachioed interpreter, according to Higgins, "can learn a language in a fortnight—knows dozens of them. A sure mark of a fool. As a phonetician, no good whatever." He is completely fooled by Liza's performance as a lady of high society and declares that she must be a European duchess.

Mrs. Pearce

Higgins's middle-class housekeeper. Very practical, she can be severe and is not afraid of reproaching Higgins for his lack of social graces. She is conscious of proper behavior and of her position, and quite proud. She is taken aback by the seeming impropriety of Liza coming into the Higgins household but quickly develops a bond with the girl, often defending her from Higgins.

Pick

See Colonel Pickering

Pickering

See Colonel Pickering

Colonel Pickering

A phonetics expert like Higgins, this "elderly gentleman of the amiable military type," meets the latter in a rainstorm at the St. Paul's Church. The "author of Spoken Sanskrit," Pickering excels in the Indian dialects because of his experience in the British colonies there. Courteous and generous, as well as practical and sensible, he never views Liza as just a flower girl and treats her with the respect due a lady of society. "I assure you," he responds to a challenge by Mrs. Higgins, "we take Eliza very seriously." Open-hearted, he finds it easy to sympathize with others and, decidedly unlike

Higgins, is conscience-stricken when he fears he's hurt Liza.

Themes

Appearances and Reality

Pygmalion examines this theme primarily through the character of Liza, and the issue of personal identity (as perceived by oneself or by others). Social roles in the Victorian era were viewed as natural and largely fixed: there was perceived to be something inherently, fundamentally unique about a noble versus an unskilled laborer and vice versa. Liza's ability to fool society about her "real" identity raises questions about appearances. The importance of appearance and reality to the theme *of Pygmalion* is suggested by Liza's famous observation: "You see, really and truly, apart from the things anyone can pick up (the dressing and the proper way of speaking, and so on), the difference between a lady and a flower girl is not how she behaves, but how she's treated."

Topics for Further Study

- Research the history of phonetics and speech as a subject of study; does Shaw's depiction of the scientific interests of his character Higgins seem to have been well-grounded in historical precedent?

- Compare and contrast the ways in which both Liza and her father are thrust into the middle class (she through learning to speak "properly," he through obtaining money), and why each is not comfortable in it. Through these characters, what does Shaw seem to be saying about class distinctions?

- Contrast Colonel Pickering and Henry Higgins in terms of manners and behavior. What are the implications of their very different treatments of Liza?

- Research the social position of women in early twentieth-century Britain (economic opportunities, cultural conventions, legal rights), and use this information to explain further why Liza is so concerned about her future following the conclusion of Higgins's "experiment."

Beauty

In *Pygmalion,* Shaw interrogates beauty as a subjective value. One's perception of beauty in another person is shown to be a highly complex matter, dependent on a large number of (not always aesthetic) factors. Liza, it could be argued, is the same person from the beginning of the play to the end, but while she is virtually invisible to Freddy as a Cockney-speaking flower merchant, he is totally captivated by what he perceives as her beauty and grace when she is presented to him as a lady of society.

Change and Transformation

The transformation of Liza is, of course, central to the plot and theme of *Pygmalion.* The importance at first appears to rest in the power

Higgins expresses by achieving this transformation. "But you have no idea," he says, "how frightfully interesting it is to take a human being and change her into a quite different human being by creating a new speech for her. It's filling up the deepest gulf that separates class from class and soul from soul." As the play unfolds, however, the focus shifts so that the effects of the change upon Liza become central. The truly important transformation Liza goes through is not the adoption of refined speech and manners but the learning of independence and a sense of inner self-worth that allows her to leave Higgins.

Identity

The indeterminacy of appearance and reality in *Pygmalion* reveals the significant examination of identity in the play. Shaw investigates conflicts between differing perceptions of identity and depicts the end result of Higgins's experiment as a crisis of identity for Liza. Liza's transformation is glorious but painful, as it leaves her displaced between her former social identity and a new one, which she has no income or other resources to support. Not clearly belonging to a particular class, Liza no longer knows *who she is*.

Language and Meaning

In an age of growing standardization of what was known as "the Queen's English," *Pygmalion* points to a much wider range of varieties of spoken

English. Shaw believed characteristics of social identity such as one's refinement of speech were completely subjective ones, as his play suggests. While Shaw himself hated poor speech and the varieties of dialect and vocabulary could present obstructions to conveying meaning, nevertheless the play suggests that the real richness of the English language is in the variety of individuals who speak it. As for the dialect or vocabulary of any one English variety, such as Cockney, its social value is determined in *Pygmalion* completely by the context in which it is assessed. While Liza's choice of words as a Cockney flower merchant would be thought as absurd as her accent, they are later perceived by the mannered Eynsford Hill family to be the latest trend, when they are thought to emanate from a person of noble breeding.

Sex Roles

Sex and gender have a great deal to do with the dynamics between Liza and Higgins, including the sexual tension between them that many audience members would have liked to see fulfilled through a romantic union between them. In Liza's difficult case, what are defined as her options are clearly a limited subset of options available to a woman. As Mrs. Higgins observes, after the conclusion of the experiment Liza will have no income, only "the manners and habits that disqualify a fine lady from earning her own living." To this problem Higgins can only awkwardly suggest marriage to a rich man as a solution. Liza makes an astute observation about Higgins's suggestion, focusing on the limited options available to a woman: "I sold flowers. I didn't sell myself. Now you've made a lady of me I'm not fit to sell anything else."

Ubermensch ("Superman")

Shaw's belief in the Life Force and the possibility of human evolution on an individual or social level led him to believe also in the possibility of the Superman, a realized individual living to the fullest extent of his or her capacity. (The naming of the concept is credited to the influential German philosopher Friedrich Wilhelm Nietzsche, 1844-1900). Shaw addresses the topic explicitly in his play *Man and Superman* and in many other works, but he also approaches it in *Pygmalion*. Higgins, for example, represents the height of scientific achievement in his field, though he may be too flawed as an individual to continue evolving towards a superhuman level. Liza, proving herself capable of one type of transformation, also makes an important step towards self-awareness and self-realization, which for Shaw is the beginning of almost endless possibilities for personal development.

Wealth and Poverty

One of the many subjects under examination in *Pygmalion* is class consciousness, a concept first given name in 1887. Shaw's play, like so many of his writings, examines both the realities of class and its subjective markers. The linguistic signals of social identity, for example, are simultaneously an issue of class. Economic issues are central to Liza's crisis at the conclusion of Higgins's experiment, for she lacks the means to maintain the standard of living he and Pickering enjoy. Doolittle's unforeseen rise into the middle class similarly allows Shaw to examine wealth and poverty. Though Doolittle fears the workhouse he's not happy with his new class identity, either; Shaw injects humor through Doolittle's surprising (according to traditional class values) distaste for his new status.

Plotting with a Purpose

In *Pygmalion's* plot, Higgins, a phonetics expert, makes a friendly bet with his colleague Colonel Pickering that he can transform the speech and manners of Liza, a common flower girl, and present her as a lady to fashionable society. He succeeds, but Liza gains independence in the process, and leaves her former tutor because he is incapable of responding to her needs.

Pygmalion has a tightly-constructed plot, rising conflict, and other qualities of the "well-made play," a popular form at the time. Shaw, however, revolutionized the English stage by disposing of other conventions of the well-made play; he discarded its theatrical dependence on prolonging and then resolving conflict in a sometimes contrived manner for a theater of ideas grounded in realism. Shaw was greatly influenced by Henrik Ibsen, who he claimed as a forerunner to his theatre of discussion or ideas. Ibsen's *A Doll House,* Shaw felt, was an example of how to end a play indeterminately, leading the audience to reflect upon character and theme, rather than simply entertaining them with a neatly-resolved conclusion.

Intellect vs. Entertainment

Shaw broke both with the predominant intellectual principle of his day, that of "art for art's sake," as well as with the popular notion that the purpose of the theatre was strictly to entertain. Refusing to write a single sentence for the sake of either art or entertainment alone, Shaw openly declared that he was for a theater which preached to its audience on social issues. Edward Wagenknecht wrote in *A Guide to Bernard Shaw* that Shaw's plays "are not plays: they are tracts in dramatic form." He further reflected a popular perception of Shaw's plays as intellectual exercises by stating that Shaw "has created one great character—G.B.S. [George Bernard Shaw]—and in play after play he performs infinite variations upon it." Thus, in his day Shaw was viewed as succeeding *despite* his dramatic technique rather than because of it. Wagenknecht again: "it is amazing that a man whose theory of art is so patently wrong should have achieved such a place as Shaw has won."

Though his plays do tend towards ideological discussion rather than dramatic tension, Shaw succeeded because he nevertheless understood what made a play theatrical, wrote scintillating dialogue, and always created rich, complex characters in the center of a philosophically complex drama. Among his character creations are some of the greatest in the modern theatre, especially the women: Major Barbara, Saint Joan, Liza Doolittle. Also, Shaw's deep belief in the need for social improvement did not prevent him from having a wry sense of humor, an additional component of his dramatic technique which helped his plays, *Pygmalion* most predominantly, bridge a gap between popular and intellectual art.

Romance

In calling *Pygmalion* a *romance* (its subtitle is "A Romance in Five Acts"), Shaw was referencing a well-established literary form (not usually employed in theatre), to which *Pygmalion* does not fully conform. (Shaw was aiming to provoke thought by designating his play thusly.) The term romance does not imply, as it was misinterpreted to mean by many of Shaw's contemporaries, a romantic element between Liza and Higgins. Since the middle ages, romances have been distinguished from more realistic forms by their exotic, exaggerated narratives, and their idealized characters and themes. Shaw playfully suggests *Pygmalion* is a romance because of the almost magical transformations which occur in the play and the idealized qualities to which the characters aspire.

Historical Context

World War I

Nineteen-fourteen, the year of *Pygmalion's* London premiere, marked tremendous changes in British society. On July 28, the Austrian archduke Franz Ferdinand and his wife were assassinated in Sarajevo, Bosnia, setting off an international conflict due to a complicated set of alliances which had developed in Europe. Within two weeks, this conflict had erupted into a world war (known in Britain at the time as the "Great War"). By the end of World War I (as it came to be known later), 8.5 million people had been killed and 21 million wounded, including significant civilian casualties. The war constituted the most intense physical, economic and psychological assault on European society in its history; Britain was not alone in experiencing devastating effects on its national morale and other aspects of society.

It is ironic, Eldon C. Hill wrote in *George Bernard Shaw,* that *Pygmalion,* "written partly to demonstrate that language (phonetics particularly) could contribute to understanding among men, should be closed because of the outbreak of World War I." The war brought out Shaw's compassion, as well as his disgust with the European societies that would tolerate the destruction of so many lives. When the actress Mrs. Patrick Campbell informed

Shaw of the death of her son in battle, he replied that he could not be sympathetic, but only furious: "Killed just because people are blasted fools," Hill quoted the playwright saying. To Shaw, the war only demonstrated more clearly the need for human advancement on an individual and social level, to reach a level of understanding that would prevent such tragic devastation.

Colonialism and the British Empire

In 1914 Great Britain was very much still a colonial power, but while victory in the First World War actually increased the size of the British Empire, the war itself simultaneously accelerated the development of nationalism and autonomy in the provinces. Even before the war, British pride in its Empire had reached a climax prior to the death of Queen Victoria in 1901, and the brutalities of the Boer War (1899-1902), fought to assert Britain's authority in South Africa. Still, British society proudly proclaimed that "the sun never sets on the British Empire" and believed in Britain's providential mission in geographies as widely diverse as Ireland, Australia and New Zealand, India, Burma, Egypt, the Sudan, South Africa, Nigeria, Guyana, Honduras, Jamaica, and numerous other islands throughout the Caribbean, and Canada.

Compare & Contrast

- **1910s:** Women in Britain do not

have the right to vote, and their opportunities for education and employment remain limited.

Today: Since 1928, all women over the age of 21 have had the right to vote in Britain. The direct participation of women in government continues to be more limited than that of men, although the election of Margaret Thatcher as Prime Minister in 1979 set an important precedent. Women were admitted to full admission at Oxford in 1920 and to Cambridge University in 1948. Women make up a much larger portion of the work force than they did at the turn of the century, and although their compensation and employment opportunities continue to lag behind those of men, the Equal Pay Act of 1970 and other measures have addressed this issue. It is no longer the case that a women's natural role is widely assumed to be limited to domestic work.

- **1910s:** With industrialization and legislative reform beginning a process of diversification, Britain's society is still rigidly hierarchical, with a tradition of a landed aristocracy and a pyramid of descending ranks and degrees. In 1911, the power of the royally-appointed House of Lords in Parliament to veto the legislation of the democratically-elected House of Commons is reduced to a power to delay legislation.

Today: The political power of royalty and the nobility has been greatly reduced through a process of legislative reform. While titles of nobility remain, Britain's society remains stratified primarily by wealth rather than rank. While the middle class grew considerably throughout the century and there was significant growth in economic indicators such as owner-occupation of homes, sharp divisions between rich and poor persist in Britain. With the growth of the technical institutes, the "polytechnics," the expansion of the university system after World War II greatly increased opportunities for higher education in the country.

- **1910s:** Despite the promotion of a standard "Queen's English," beginning in the Victorian era, the British Isles—even London itself—is marked by a wide diversity of spoken English. The diversity of

British population (including its varieties of English) was further shaped by large-scale immigration, by Irish beginning in the 1830s, Germans in the 1840s, Scandinavians in the 1870s, and Eastern Europeans in the 1880s.

Today: The diversity of English culture—especially in London and the major cities—has been further increased, along with the diversity of English dialects, by twentieth-century immigration from Britain's colonies and former colonies in Africa, the Caribbean, the Indian subcontinent, and the Far East.

- **1910s:** Europe is devastated by the 8.5 million dead and 21 million wounded in "the Great War" (World War I), including unprecedented levels of civilian casualties. Britain was not alone in experiencing the most intense physical, economic, and psychological assault in its history.

Today: The specter of civilian death leads to a realization that modern warfare potentially endangers the future of the entire nation. This feeling has been accentuated since the end of World War II by the threat of nuclear destruction. Much more so than at the beginning of the century, citizens have come to perceive war and the necessity of avoiding it as their business, and they often try to impact their government's policies to this end. Shaw's position against war, still somewhat radical in his day, has become much more common.

In addition to providing a symbolic unity to the Empire, the long reign of Queen Victoria (1837-1901) also gave coherence to British society at home, through a set of values known as Victorianism. Victorian values revolved around social high-mindedness (a Christian sense of charity and service), domesticity (most education and entertainment occurred in the home, but children, who "should be seen and not heard," were reared with a strict hand) and a confidence in the expansion of knowledge and the power of reasoned argument to change society. By the time of Victoria's death, many of the more traditional mid-Victorian values were already being challenged, as was the class structure upon which many of these values depended. Victorianism, however, survived in a modified form through the reign of Victoria's son, Edward. 1914, the year of *Pygmalion* and the onset of the Great War, constituted a much different kind of break, symbolic and social.

Industrialization

The growth of industrialization throughout the nineteenth century had a tremendous impact on the organization of British society, which had (much more so than the United States) a tradition of a landed aristocracy and a more hierarchical class system—a pyramid of descending ranks and degrees. Allowing for the growth of a merchant middle class, industrialization changed British society into a plutocracy—an aristocracy of money more than land. Social mobility, however, still did not widely extend into the lower classes, propagating a lack of opportunity reflected in Liza's anxiety over what is to happen to her following Higgins's experiment.

Industrialization brought about a demographic shift throughout the nineteenth century, with more and more agricultural laborers coming to seek work in the cities. Unskilled laborers like the Doolittles competed for limited employment amid the poverty of the inner city and were largely at the mercy of employers. Increased health standards combated urban crises like tuberculosis and cholera, but slum conditions and rampant urban poverty remained a major social problem after the turn of the century. *Pygmalion* suggests the subjectivity of class identity, and the rapid deterioration of many pre-industri-al social structures, but strict class distinctions of another kind nevertheless persisted. This fact is suggested by the severely disproportionate distribution of wealth in Britain at the time: during the years 1911-1913, the top 1% of the population controlled 65.5% of the nation's capital. The poorest of the poor, meanwhile, were often forced into workhouses, institutions which had been developed in the 17th century to employ paupers and the indigent at profitable work. Conditions in the workhouses differed little from prisons; they were deliberately harsh and degrading in order to discourage the poor from relying upon them. Conditions in the workhouses improved later in the 19th century but were still unpleasant enough that fear of going to one, for example, causes Doolittle in *Pygmalion* to accept his new position in the middle class even though it is displeasing to him for other reasons.

The Rise of Women and the Working Classes

During the decade which produced *Pygmalion,* the political power of the working class increased greatly, through massive increases in trade union membership. Bitter class divisions gave rise to waves of strikes and disturbances, including a major railway strike in 1911, a national miners' strike in 1912, and the "Triple Alliance" of miners, railway, and transport workers in 1914. A new political party, Labour, came into existence in 1893, advancing an eight-hour work day and other workplace reforms. Meanwhile, reforms to laws concerning suffrage, the right to vote, further brought men (and later, women) of the working class into Britain's ever-more participatory democracy. Suffrage (the right to vote) had in Britain always been based on requirements of property ownership, reflecting the contemporary idea that only landowners were considered reasoned and informed enough to vote but also that they would do so in the best interest of those in the classes below them. These property requirements were gradually relaxed throughout the nineteenth century, gradually increasing the size of the male electorate.

Only after many years of political struggle by organizations of women known as "suffragettes" did women achieve the right to vote: first in 1918 for women over 30 who also met a requirement of property ownership, then extended in 1928 to all women over the age of 21 (as was already the case for men). Increased political participation further prompted a shift in sex roles: British society had already noted the phenomenon of "the new woman," and was to see further changes such as increasing numbers of women in the work force, as well as reforms to divorce laws and other impacts upon domestic life.

Critical Overview

Building upon the acclaim *Pygmalion* had received from German-language production and publication, the original English production of the play at His Majesty's Theatre was likewise a success, securing Shaw's reputation as a popular playwright. Still, contemporary reviews of *Pygmalion* are mixed, revealing the somewhat prejudicial views English critics continue to hold towards Shaw's work. For example, an unsigned review in the *Westminster Gazette,* reprinted in *Shaw: The Critical Heritage,* criticized many aspects of the production but had qualified praise for the play, "a puzzling work." Aware that Shaw usually "does not use the drama merely as a vehicle for telling stories," the critic expressed a curiosity about what "the foundation idea" of *Pygmalion* might be. "Curiosity, in the present instance," however, "remains unsatisfied. There are plenty of ideas, but none is predominant."

Alex M. Thompson, meanwhile, wrote in a review in the *Clarion* that "Britain's most famous playwright has won his place at last on the stage of Britain's most famous playhouse" but regretted that "while the great playwright's really significant plays" were wasted through production elsewhere, "the play admitted to our classic shrine is one whose purpose, according to the author himself, is 'to boil the pot.'" H. W. Massingham, in a review for the *Nation,* declared that "there is a fault in the piece as well as in its production," namely that Shaw "observes too coldly": in pursuing the clash of wits, the excitement of argument, he obscures real beauty and affection. Shaw, somewhat like Higgins, "hides his spirituality or his tenderness under a mask of coarseness," to the extent that he "has failed to show his audience precisely what he meant."

The sensation caused by Shaw's use of the mild profanity "bloody" (breaking with tradition at His Majesty's Theatre) went a long way to ensure the publicity for *Pygmalion,* but many critics found the language of the play shocking. T. F. Evans commented in his notes for *Shaw: The Critical Heritage,* that "[it] is almost impossible . . . to assess accurately the critical response to the play itself because of the totally disproportionate amount of space, time and attention that was given to the use by Shaw . . . of the word 'bloody'. . . . Some critics who might have been expected to give largely favourable comments on the play seem to have allowed the use of the adjective to affect them." By 1938, however, the year *Pygmalion* was made into a movie, Shaw's text was still dramatic and challenging but much of the shock had faded. Of the film version, Desmond MacCarthy observed in *Shaw: The Plays* that "'bloody' still gets its laugh, but it no longer releases the roar that greets the crash of a taboo."

In his 1929 study *A Guide to Bernard Shaw,* Edward Wagenknecht demonstrated the delicate balance many critical interpretations of Shaw in that era tried to maintain, explaining how Shaw had succeeded despite breaking many established conventions of dramatic art. Shaw "revolted" against deeply-held ideas that literature is writing which supersedes a specific purpose other than to communicate life experience, and is not didactic. "It is amazing," Wagenknecht wrote, "that a man whose theory of art is so patently wrong should have achieved such a place as Shaw has won."

By the end of Shaw's life, his status as perhaps the greatest single English dramatist since Shakespeare was secure, but nevertheless critical opinion on him appeared mixed and in many cases prejudiced. Eric Bentley wrote in his book *Bernard Shaw, 1856-1950,* that in reviewing the already voluminous writing on Shaw, "I found praise, but most of it naive or invidious. I found blame, but most of it incoherent and scurrilous." Perhaps Shaw's complexity of thought provoked these mixed (and largely unsatisfying) critical assessments, to the extent that to some critics "Shaw, the champion of will and feeling, is an arch-irrationalist," but to others "Shaw, the champion and incarnation of intellect, is the arch-rationalist." In *Pygmalion* Bentley found a play of "singularly elegant structure . . . a good play by perfectly orthodox standards" needing "no theory to defend it."

In his summary of the play's merits, Bentley avoided the tendency of earlier critics to distinguish sharply between various aspects of Shaw's work, instead celebrating the intimate connection between them. *Pygmalion,* he wrote, "is Shavian, not in being made up of political or philosophic discussions, but in being based on the standard conflict of vitality and system, in working out this conflict through an inversion of romance, in bringing matters to a head in a battle of wills and words, in having an inner psychological action in counterpoint to the outer romantic action . . . in delighting and surprising us with a constant flow of verbal music and more than verbal wit." Bentley's modern assessment of the complexity of Shaw's political thought and dramatic method established a precedent for much Shavian criticism of the last fifty years.

Beginning immediately with the first English production of *Pygmalion,* a popular debate developed as to whether there should have been a romantic ending between Higgins and Liza. Shaw insisted that such an ending would have been misery for his characters but producers and audiences nevertheless tended to prefer a romantic ending. MacCarthy expressed the sentiments of many when he wrote about the original production "when the curtain fell on the mutual explanations of this pair [Higgins and Liza] I was in a fever to see it rise on Acts VI and VII; I wanted to see those two living together."

When the play was first published in 1916, Shaw added an afterword which recounted what Liza did after leaving Higgins and was intended to show to audiences that there was to be "no sentimental nonsense" about the possibility of Higgins and Liza being lovers. The English-language film of *Pygmalion* gave Shaw another opportunity to remove "virtually every suggestion of Higgins's possible romantic interest in Liza." He was to discover, however, at a press show two days before the film's premiere, that the director had hired other screenwriters who added a "sugar-sweet ending" in which Higgins and Liza are united as lovers. MacCarthy commented in 1938 that the effect of the changes in the film version "is merely that of a wish fulfillment love story of a poor girl who became a lady and married the man who made her one." He observes that the difference is "due to a peculiarity inherent in the art of cinema itself (a need for closure), and that the changed ending is no doubt what accounts for the film's "immense popularity."

Sources

Berst, Charles A. *Bernard Shaw and the Art of Drama* University of Illinois Press (Urbana), 1973, pp. 197-218.

Further Reading

Bentley, Eric. *Bernard Shaw, 1856-1950,* amended edition, New Directions, 1957.

> Though Bentley's book (originally published in 1947) is not adulatory, Shaw considered it "the best book written about himself as a dramatist." Bentley states that his double intention in the book is "to disentangle a credible man and artist from the mass of myth that surrounds him, and to discover the complex component parts of his 'simplicity.'" *Pygmalion* is discussed in detail, pages 119-126, and elsewhere in the book.

Crane, Milton. *"Pygmalion:* Bernard Shaw's Dramatic Theory and Practice" in *Publications of the Modern Language Association,* Vol. 66, no.6, December, 1951, pp. 879-85.

> Crane begins with the question of whether Shaw was old-fashioned in his approach to drama or innovative. Wrapped up in this issue is the figure of Ibsen, who Shaw declared was revolutionary for giving his plays indeterminate endings and concluding with "discussion," rather than the clear unraveling of a

dramatic situation in the "well-made play"—the popular form of the day. Crane demonstrates that Ibsen did not present a new innovation so much as modify earlier forms and claims that something similar holds true for Shaw as well. Although Shaw denied his audience a romantic ending in *Pygmalion,* Crane does not feel it is true of the playwright what many have said, "that he is primarily a thinker, who chose for rhetorical reasons to cast his ideas in dramatic form." Rather than viewing his characters abstractly, as means to a rhetorical end, Shaw was passionately invested in their lives and destinies, which highlights a basic "conventionality" in his technique.

Dukore, Bernard F. "The Director As Interpreter: Shaw's *Pygmalion"* in *Shaw,* Vol. 3, 1983, pp. 129-47.

A three-part article analyzing, first, "Shaw's concept of the question of directorial interpretation"; then his own directorial interpretation of *Pygmalion* (in the London premiere and several subsequent productions); and finally, the revisions he made to *Pygmalion* as a result of the experience of directing the play.

Dukore shows the careful separation Shaw maintained between "Playwright Shaw" and "Director Shaw": rather than explain to his actors the ideas in his play in a literary manner, Shaw was able to help them in very practical terms to develop their performances. Often these actors led him to new insights about his own characters. "While he recognized that there are a variety of appropriate ways to interpret any well-written role," however, Shaw also "rejected what he considered inappropriate interpretations."

Evans, T. F., editor. *Shaw: The Critical Heritage,* Routledge & Kegan Paul (London), 1976.

An extremely useful collection of 135 contemporary writings on Shaw's plays: reviews, essays, letters, and other sources. Arranged roughly in chronological order and grouped by play, the items "give a continuing picture of the changing and developing reaction to Shaw's dramatic work." *Pygmalion* is covered on pages 223-29.

Harvey, Robert C. "How Shavian is the *Pygmalion* We Teach?" in *English Journal,* Vol. 59, 1970, pp. 1234-38.

This article by a former high school

English teacher begins with the observation that while Shaw lived, he absolutely refused to let his plays be published in school textbooks: "My plays were not designed as instruments of torture," he wittily commented. Harvey recognizes that despite the wishes of the playwright, there are definite values to students reading his work in a school setting. Too often, however, the work is taught to support grammar lessons, with the message that like Liza, students can succeed if they learn to speak "correctly." Harvey affirms that the real value of the piece for students is in trying to grasp its literary complexity. If anything, the play should show students "the social importance of all varieties of language . . . the equality of every dialect" rather than being used "to forge the very chains [Shaw] wrote the play to break."

Henderson, Archibald. *George Bernard Shaw: Man of the Century,* Appleton-Century-Crofts (New York), 1956.

A final, culminating book by Shaw's "official" biographer, incorporating much material from his previous works. Henderson studied Shaw first-hand and wrote on him for over fifty years.

Hill, Eldon C. *George Bernard Shaw,* Twayne (Boston), 1978.

> A biography and critical study intended not for the Shaw specialist but for the general reader "who seeks an understanding of Shaw's life and work." *Pygmalion* is discussed in detail, pages 118-21.

Huggett, Richard. *The Truth about* Pygmalion, Heinemann (London), 1969.

> Focusing predominantly on Mrs. Patrick Campbell, the actress who created Liza for the London premiere, this study is the result of three years of research into the play and its performances.

Kaufman, R. J., editor. *G. B. Shaw: A Collection of Critical Essays,* Prentice-Hall (Englewood Cliffs, NJ), 1965.

> While none of the essays examines *Pygmalion* exclusively, the topics of these compiled studies overlap extensively with issues in that particular play. Notable contributions include a short, provocative piece by Bertolt Brecht, showing Shaw's influence on his work. Brecht states of Shaw's view towards society, "it should be clear by now that Shaw is

a terrorist. The Shavian terror is an unusual one, and he employs an unusual weapon—that of humor." In his article "Born to Set It Right: The Roots of Shaw's Style," Richard M. Ohmann investigates the development of Shaw's position as a social outsider, "the critic of things as they are." Eric Bentley's "The Making of a Dramatist" examines the formative years 1892-1903 in Shaw's life.

MacCarthy, Desmond. *Shaw: The Plays,* Newton Abbott, 1951.

Originally published as a series of essays from 1907 to 1950, this book offers a unique chance to trace the development of a particular perspective on Shaw's long and prolific career. *Pygmalion* is discussed in detail, pages 108-13.

Miller, Jane M. "Some Versions of *Pygmalion"* in *Ovid Renewed: Ovidian Influences on Literature and Art from the Middle Ages to the Twentieth Century,* edited by Charles Martindale, Cambridge University Press, 1988.

A study of Ovid's version of the *Pygmalion* myth (including possible antecedents for it), and its influence on later works. Miller stresses the sexual implications of the

Pygmalion-Galatea relationship in Ovid's story (which suggest possible consequences for Shaw's version). Miller states that the various versions of Pygmalion tend in general to be of two types: historical, which depict a social transformation and which usually contain "an element of social comment" (she places Shaw's *Pygmalion* in this category); and mystical, which explore "love as a divine experience." Miller suggests Shakespeare's *The Winter's Tale* as an early example of the "mystical" interpretation but comments that the form abounded in the nineteenth century in particular. Miller concludes that the "historicist" versions of Pygmalion, Shaw's included, "are interesting products of their time but lack the vitality of the Ovidian original."

Muggleston, Lynda. "Shaw, Subjective Inequality, and the Social Meanings of Language in *Pygmalion*" in *Review of English Studies: A Quarterly Journal of English Literature and the English Language,* Vol. 44, no. 175, August, 1993, pp. 373-85.

A detailed study of the social importance of *Pygmalion's* exploration of accent and pronunciation as determiners "not only of social status but also of social acceptability." Although difficult only in places for readers not familiar with some linguistic vocabulary, the article's central argument is easily grasped: that Shaw rebelled against the idea that there was something inherently better about people of the upper classes and therefore demonstrated that social judgments of a person's merit depend on superficial, subjective qualities (like proper speech). *Pygmalion* is a "paradigm of social mobility," illustrating that social transformation is possible, and "a paean to inherent equality," suggesting that a person's merit is distinct and separate from their level of social acceptability.

Quinn, Martin. "The Informing Presence of Charles Dickens in Bernard Shaw's *Pygmalion*" in the *Dickensian,* Vol. 80, no. 3, Autumn, 1984, pp. 144-50.

This article traces a number of connections between *Pygmalion* and various works of Dickens, who Quinn states "entered Shaw's life early and completely and was thereafter always at his fingertips when not on the tip of his tongue." Quinn shows that Dickens was specifically on Shaw's mind when writing *Pygmalion* in 1912, because he was completing at the same time an introduction to Dickens's novel *Hard Times*. The influence of Dickens was "pervasive" throughout Shaw's career, however. The value of Quinn's article is in documenting the exhaustive reading of "[a]n intellect as comprehensive as Shaw's," and inserting the name of Dickens, a novelist, among the list of dramatic artists considered to be Shaw's major influences: Shakespeare, Moliere, and Ibsen.

Shaw Bulletin, Shaw Review, Shaw: The Annual of Bernard Shaw Studies, the *Shavian.*

Publications of the Shaw Society of America *(The Shaw Bulletin,* 1952-1958; *Shaw Review,* 1951-1980; and the *Shaw* annual, 1981-present) and the Shaw Society, London (the *Shavian,* 1953-present). These journals have published extensively on all topics related to Shaw's work; check their title and subject indexes for further information.

Small, Barbara J. "Shaw on Standard Stage Speech" in *Shaw Review,* Vol. 22, 1979, pp. 106-13.

A short but enlightening study of Shaw's interest in diction and stage speech. Not entirely about *Pygmalion,* but its references to that play suggest the close relationship between Higgins and Shaw's own ideals of spoken speech. "Shaw was preoccupied with the dearth of good standard speech on the English stage," Small wrote. "Good diction was, for Shaw, associated with fine acting." Shaw did not blame individuals for their poor pronunciation; in his preface to *Pygmalion,* for example, he decries the problems stemming from English not being a language with phonetic spellings of words. These larger issues Shaw addressed through a phonetic system of his own devising, and other means, but regarding individual persons what Shaw hated most was pretension. "An honest slum dialect" was preferable to him "than the attempts of phonetically untaught persons to imitate the plutocracy."

Wagenknecht, Edward. *A Guide to Bernard Shaw,* Russell & Russell (New York), 1929.

A study written while Shaw was alive and at the peak of his career (he had won the Nobel Prize only a few years previously). Wagenknecht wrote that the purpose of his book is expository rather than critical: that is, "to gather together . . . all the information which, in my judgment, the student or general reader needs to have in mind in order to read Shaw's plays intelligently." As a study, it has largely been superseded by other later works, but it remains an important historical document.